Mediation

Conflict Management and Resolution

by

Valentin Boyadzhiev
member of
ISAP, АБПП and IAHT

"If they didn't argue with each other, they don't know each other."

***

"The more we run away from conflicts, the more they get over us."

***

"The more we try to avoid them, the more they control us."

***

"The less we fear conflicts, the less they confuse us."

***

"The less we deny our differences, the less they divide us."

Content

Introduction...................................…..…7

About the author…………………..……10

What is mediation?…………………....12

Comparison between the mediation process and the court trial……………………..15

Comparison between the basic techniques and methods in mediation and court trial……………………………………20

What is it like to be a mediator………….24

The three columns of mediation…………..27

The phases of mediation……………...…28

Types of decisions in mediation…..……33

Stages of escalation of conflicts……...…36

"The ability to communicate"……………40

What is communication?………………42

The skill of leading a conversation………48

Techniques for leading a conversation…..52

Techniques for asking questions………...56

"Reflecting team"………………………..64

Small group work. Practical exercise…...76

Final Words……………………………..82

Introduction

Ladies and Gentlemen, It is my pleasure to present you with the book "**Mediation: Conflict Management and Resolution**". The book is pleasant and easily accessible for each of you. It is packed with accessible information that you can use in your daily life as well as in your professional field. Conflicts are all around us. Rarely, almost never, will you meet a person who can boast that he has never come into conflict with another person. It's not dangerous and scary to get into a dispute, it's scary not knowing how to get out of it!

This book will give you clear guidance and understanding of the stages of the conflict, the methods of solution, the possible outcomes and more.

Mediation, in turn, is an elegant tool for resolving multiple and diverse conflict situations. It is used in various fields of social and professional life. There are also people who have made mediation their way of life and their profession.

This book might not make you a mediator, it might not teach you everything about this profession or professional field of expression, but it could introduce you to its subject, the sphere of influence and highlights, and would certainly be useful in your daily routine and when resolving another dispute, debate, or conflict with another person.

The book will cover 15 topics:
1. What is mediation?
2. Comparison between mediation and court trial.

3. Comparison between the basic techniques and methods in mediation and court trial.

4. What is it like to be a mediator?

5. The three columns of mediation.

6. The phases of mediation.

7. Types of decisions in mediation.

8. Stages of escalation of conflicts.

9. "The ability to communicate"

10. What is communication?

11. The skill of leading a conversation.

12. Techniques for leading a conversation.

13. Techniques for asking questions.

14. "Reflecting Team"

15. Small group work. Practical exercise.

About the author

Valentin Boyadzhiev is a trained nutritionist, graduated Master of Psychology in "Psychology and Psychopathology of Development". He has acquired Professional Qualification "Teacher of Psychology" and Postgraduate Professional Qualification "Psychological Counseling in Psychosomatic and Social Adaptation Disorders". He has obtained a Psychoanalysis Diploma and he has specialized in Psychoanalytic Psychotherapy. He is a member of the Association "Bulgarian Psychoanalytic Space", "International Society of Applied Psychoanalysis" and „International Alliance of Holistic Therapists". He is a lecturer on issues related to nutrition, diet, supplementation, food, and sports. He is also a teacher and a lecturer in the field of psychology, logic, ethics, law, and philosophy. He has been a school psychologist since 2017. He has been participating annually in scientific conferences on psychology, psychotherapy, dietetics, and medicine. His main interest and practice are in the field of psychoanalysis and clinical psychology.

What is mediation?

Mediation is a form of conflict resolution in which all parties have the opportunity to present their views to an impartial third party who, through a purposeful, structured conversation process, makes a joint decision of the conflict possible. The purpose of mediation is to resolve a conflict by jointly finding a solution by interested parties. They need to find a way to communicate with each other in the future without help. In the process of mediation, skills must be developed through which future conflicts could be handled and resolved.

The main principles of mediation are:

Voluntariness
Personal responsibility

Awareness
Confidentiality

History of mediation:

Mediation has existed for a long time and is present in one way or another in all cultures. We would even say that some of these cultures have had a mediating character. The so-called "Mediation committees" have existed in Japan and China for over a thousand years. The ancient philosopher Confucius shared and spread an attitude that bore a great resemblance to some elements of today's mediation. Socrates advocated the so-called mayeutics, ie. the method by which ideas are "born". According to him, knowledge is not the property of a higher authority but is "born" through joint efforts and reflection. Palaver is becoming an African mediation method in which prominent people are participants in the conflict. Contarini, a

Venetian, was explicitly listed as a "mediator" at the end of the Thirty Years' War in the 1648 Peace Treaty after many years of mediation between the parties to the conflict. In 1803, after The Stecklikrieg civil war ("War of Sticks"), Napoleon Bonaparte signed the so-called "Act of Mediation" (French: Acte de Médiation). In the 20th century, the term mediation was officially used in the Federal Mediation and Conciliation Service. The first Neighborhood Justice Centers were established in the 1970s. Since 1945, mediation has been enshrined in the Charter of the United Nations (also known as the UN Charter). In the 1980s, the concept of mediation began to take hold in Europe. It is reflected in many European laws.

Comparison between the mediation process and the court trial

The principle of delegation is firmly established in the court trial. This principle represents the possibility of the parties to be represented by lawyers. These lawyers accordingly defend the client's position and accept it as their own. Also, the participation of the parties is weak. Another key point in the trial is that **justice rules sovereignly**, ie. a third party (the court, or in particular the judge) decides what the outcome of the process will be. In the trial, each of the parties concerned considers that is "entitled to ...", i.e. **each party defends its own position** by defending its own rights and seeking justice. Here we come to a point that we can call **a struggle for justice**. Each party is involved in this struggle, and will inevitably lead to either **victory or loss**. In a court trial, **decisions are of the "either, or" type**, ie. there is no way both sides can win and receive what they want. Also, in order for a court trial to be accomplished, **the conflict must necessarily be or become real**, ie. no trial can be held if the conflict is only in the imagination of one of the parties. **Conflict resolution comes only at the end of the whole process**, ie. it is necessary to go through a long procedure in order to reach a judgment by the court dealing with the conflict. Unfortunately, a lawsuit inevitably leads to a point where **the weaknesses of one or the other party (if not both) are used as a weapon against them**. Another potential negative observed in the trial is the possibility that **the development of the process will be "frozen"**. There is also **no room for learning in the trial**, ie neither side has the opportunity to learn from mistakes, to gain certain knowledge, to develop new communication skills and so on. **In litigation, the only reference system is the law**, ie. the decision cannot have anything to do with personal opinions, feelings and emotions. Also, **the time and speed of the process are almost impossible to calculate**.

Unlike the court process, in mediation **the principle of personal responsibility** is strongly advocated, ie. a person expresses his own points of view, feelings, experiences, desires and so on. Another difference is that **justice is developed by the parties themselves**, ie. the mediator does not have the right to make decisions (unlike the court and the judge in the trial). In the mediation process, **the interests and needs of both parties are at the forefront**, ie. solutions are sought that satisfy both parties to the maximum extent. Here the so-called **"Art of Peace"** is fully realized and all opportunities and conditions for **cooperation** are used, ie. an agreement is sought between the parties. The aim is to find **solutions of type "and"** that satisfy both parties. In mediation, **the dynamics of the relationship and emotions can be seen** and often discussed and understood. In this process, **weaknesses are not used from the parties as weapons against each other** in the conflict. Also, mediation allows us to discover new moments important for the parties and to discover and discuss the underlying concerns, fears, worries and so on. Here we need to mention one of the main positives of this type of process, namely **the ability to learn**, ie. the opportunity to acquire new knowledge, skills and competencies to be used to resolve future conflicts. In mediation, the law is not the only referent. **Other systems and subsystems can be involved** here, such as culture, religion, economy, various aspects of connection, the state of mind of the parties and others. In the mediation process, the time and speed at which the process takes place can be determined.

Comparison between the basic techniques and methods in mediation and court trial

Regarding the legal solution to the problem, we can consider some key points. **Clarification of guilt** comes to the fore, ie. whether an action was committed intentionally, inadvertently, negligently, etc. This is important for the process, as the various penalties and sanctions relate to multiple conditions, one of which is guilt. Also, the whole process is **directed (oriented) to the norm**, ie. the average, legally acceptable behaviour is sought. **The process, so to speak, is conducted and managed by a higher-ranking wise person**, and the complaint of the respective party is addressed to him (to the judge).

The results and decisions of the trial can be and often are generalized, ie. the taken decision becomes a formal argument in subsequent court cases and is disputable and may be a legal reference. **The resolution of the conflict is accomplished by a court decision**, and not by cooperation and mutual compromise of the parties. In the trial are rarely sought personal characteristics, differences, fears, worries, etc., which are related to the obvious conflict, ie. **the problem is limited**. In this process, **persuasion** is needed, ie. both parties make efforts to convince the third party (the court) of their own right.

Mediation, on the other hand, seeks mutual solutions that satisfy both parties. It has a thematic focus, ie. various topics are addressed in the course of the process, which are related to the main conflict.

Mediation also emphasizes trust in the **wisdom of the parties concerned**, ie. they themselves can and will find a solution to the conflict. **The mediation process is self-regulating**, taking into account the specifics of each party and their wishes. **The decisions taken in mediation are not universal but are solutions for individual cases.** They have no automatic influence and value in resolving other conflicts. In the process, **the different points of view of the affected parties are accepted** and a solution is sought by **reaching a consensus**. Very often in the process, there is an expansion of the problem, ie. the search for the underlying reasons for its occurrence and for resolution. The main technique in mediation is hearing.

There are various areas of application of mediation, such as politics, environmental issues and conflicts, the school environment, society as a whole, the economy, family conflicts, neighbourhood conflicts and the work world in general.

What is it like to be a mediator?

The person who will exercise his legal right to be a mediator must be accepted and respected by all parties to the conflict. It must be a person who has the confidence of the parties in the dispute or wins it and whose competence is not disputed. The mediator should not have a personal interest in the outcome of the conflict and should not seek personal benefits from it, except for the payment due to him from both parties. However, he advocates for the interests and concerns of all parties to the conflict and needs to be impartial. The mediator is responsible for the conduct and compliance with the framework of the mediation conversation, and the parties to the conflict are responsible for the content. Interruption of mediation is possible when a reasonable and/or ethically responsible solution is not found.

The main principles of the mediator are:

Impartiality
Acceptance
Recognition
Affirmation

The tasks of the mediator are diverse. He is the **guardian of the mediation process**. His responsibility is **to create and adhere to the framework of the process**. It is necessary for him **to show a respectful attitude and behaviour** to both parties to the conflict at all times. It is also necessary to have a **deep understanding of the field of communication** and to have the necessary knowledge, skills and competencies. **Absolute impartiality,**

acceptance and respect are required of him. He seeks **to adhere to the worldview of the parties, avoiding distorting** what they say. His responsibility is **to emphasize the interests behind the positions of the parties**, ie. to identify and discuss underlying needs. The mediator **actively listens, asks questions** and tries to lead the parties **to create constructive views** on the conflict. **He structures and manages the mediation process.** He is required and expected to have **a fuller and deeper understanding of the conflict, without assessing and condemning the parties** morally or ethically. One of the main points is privacy and confidentiality. Despite all these tasks facing the mediator, he is not responsible for the conflict between the parties and is not responsible for finding a solution. These responsibilities remain in the hands of the parties.

The three columns of mediation

a) Voluntariness:

The parties must have a common interest in working on the conflict and resolving it.

b) Impartiality:

The mediator shows his obligation to the point of view of each participant equally and has an interest in all, ie. showing neutrality.

c) Personal responsibility:

Everyone should be able to take care of their personality. The parties determine whether they will communicate. The notion of autonomy is clearly present here. The decision (outcome) of the conflict is in the hands of the parties.

The phases of mediation

Mediation is a structured process and its course follows a specific sequence. In the first phase of the process, **a mediation contract** is concluded. Then, in phase two, **the various conflicts are raised and the views of the parties are considered**. In phase three, **the conflicting points, interests and needs of the parties are clarified**. In phase four, **a solution to the conflict is sought**, and in the last phase, a so-called **agreement** is reached between the parties.

Phase 1: Introduction, mediation arrangements

In the first phase of the process, it is necessary to create a good atmosphere allowing communication between the parties. It is good for the participating parties to be calm, not to be afraid of what is to come and to show a desire for cooperation. The mediator tries to create an atmosphere of trust. This is followed by a brief presentation of the parties and the mediator. The available information is clarified and the mediation process itself is explained. In this phase of the process, the basic rules of communication are set: the right of everyone to speak, the prohibition to insult and the rule to tell the truth. The working hours, the rules for taking notes and the contractual relations themselves are determined. The mediator clarifies his own role and tasks. The readiness of the parties to work is being considered and efforts are being made to build trust. The mediation contract itself is concluded.

Phase 2: Raising the conflict; consideration of the views of the parties to the conflict

In the second phase of the process, additional information is gathered and each of the parties to the conflict presents its own views on the problem. Communication between the parties takes place through the mediator in order to avoid unnecessary disputes and other activities and actions that interfere with the process. The mediator, in turn, asks questions in order to clarify the various elements and points. The mediator uses the active listening technique all the time. In this phase, efforts are focused both on establishing commonalities between the parties and on differences. For the purpose of understanding, the mediator actively uses the technique of paraphrasing.

Phase 3: Clarification of the conflict, clarification of interests and needs

In the third phase of the process, special attention is paid to the interests, feelings and preliminary information submitted by the parties. The wishes of the parties are also formulated here. Systemic questions are asked and direct communication between the parties is established. In this phase, the process of development and exchange of viewpoints on the different views of the parties is monitored and managed. The mediator often interprets the statements of the parties to clarify the hidden meanings and underlying emotions, feelings, desires, fears and needs. The aim of this phase is also to discover new perspectives and opportunities.

Phase 4: Solution to the problem

Phase four brings together a variety of ideas for resolving the conflict. Then each idea is evaluated and several interesting proposals are selected. Each proposal is developed, reviewed and evaluated. The positives and negatives for each of the parties to the conflict are considered in order to reach an agreement that satisfies both parties. Here is the moment when the most essential information is attracted, ie. here is the deepest insight into the specifics of the issue. This is also where the real discussion unfolds.

Phase 5: Agreement

In phase five, the consensus is reached. It is jointly formulated and sustainable. Every agreement reached is recorded. The application of this agreement and its implications are then clarified. Finally, the agreement is signed by the participating parties.

Types of decisions in mediation

In general, there are three main types of mediation solutions:

Win-win solution:

In order to achieve this ideal solution of mediation, the needs, desires, requirements, fears and reservations of the parties to the conflict must be consistently worked on. Therefore, this result of mediation means that all interests are satisfied and all benefit the decision as much as possible.

Consensus:

Consensus ("unification") is qualitatively the best degree of finding solutions. The consensus is a thematic union without hidden or direct contradiction. This type of solution involves the high satisfaction of the participants.

Compromise:

This type of solution is achieved through the mutual acceptance of the parties to the conflict, while at the same time each of the parties receives part of what is desired. This part satisfies both parties in a certain way. This voluntary agreement is due to the withdrawal of both parties from their previous positions and the corresponding waiver of their preliminary ideas.

Mediation, of course, has its limits. It is not a universal method for resolving any conflicts, in any size, under any conditions and so on. Where there is involuntariness and/or a high willingness to escalate the conflict, a mediation process cannot take place. Where there are excessive emotional injuries and/or fixation on the past and the events in it, mediation is also not possible. When there is non-compliance with the agreed rules, strong dominant relations between the parties to the conflict or lack of willingness to cooperate, the mediation process is also severely affected and even impossible.

Stages of escalation of conflicts

We need to consider another very important point related to the mediation process, namely the possibility of escalating conflicts. This possibility is always present, and it is necessary for the mediator to keep it in mind and at the same time, it is necessary to manage (control) the process in order to avoid or limit the influence of this escalation.

The escalation of conflicts follows its own sequence and there are so-called **stages of escalation of the conflict**.

The first stage is the so-called **"fierceness"**. There are certain disagreements with a not very frequent manifestation, there is a slight tension, but still, neither one of the parties experiences nor feels what is happening as a conflict.

The second stage is the debate. Many strategies are used here to convince the interlocutor of our own opinion. At this stage, there is an escalation of disagreements to the point of dispute.

The third stage is **the provocation** or **the transition to an action**. There is no verbal communication here. There is a lack of empathy for others. The goal of the parties is to put maximum pressure on the opponent by presenting as many facts as possible.

The fourth stage is **the coalition**. Here allies are sought in the fight against the other. The issue or cause of the conflict is no longer important. Victory is honoured and it is the only thing sought.

The fifth stage is **the loss of identity**. Here the goal is to discourage the opponent, to remove the authenticity of his words, his feelings, emotions, experiences.

The sixth stage is related to the use of **threatening strategies**. This is the place and time when direct threats are used, all sorts of sanctions are applied and attempts are made to dominate and emphasize personal power.

The seventh stage is the so-called **"limited destruction"**. At this stage, attempts are made to cause severe destruction and damage to the opponent, even at the cost of some limited damage for the attacker.

The eighth stage is **disunity**. At this stage, the goal is one and the same is the destruction of the enemy, by all means, and at all costs.

The ninth last stage is **complete destruction or self-destruction**. At this final stage of the escalation of the conflict, there is a reconciliation with the personal destruction in the defeat of the enemy.

In the first three stages, it is possible to resolve the conflict in the form of "Win-Win", ie. there is the possibility of an independent solution to the conflict, in which both sides can win.

In the transition to the next three stages, it is possible to resolve the conflict in the form of "Win-Loss", ie. there is the possibility of resolving the conflict but only with help. Then just one of the parties wins.

In the transition to the last three stages, it is possible to resolve the conflict in the form of "Loss-Loss", ie. whatever the outcome is both sides lose.

"The basis of human coexistence is twofold and yet unique: the desire of each person to be recognized by others as he is or even as he can be, and the ability of people to recognize their close ones in this way."
Martin Buber

"The ability to communicate"

"To know how"

A sultan dreamed that his teeth were falling out. Immediately after waking up, he asked a dream interpreter about the meaning of the dream. "Oh, what trouble, my lord," he cried. "Every fallen tooth means the loss of your loved one." "What insolence," shouted the sultan angrily, "what are you telling me? Get out!" and gave the order: "50 hits with a stick for this shameless man!"

Another dream interpreter was summoned and brought to the sultan. Hearing the dream, he cried out, "What happiness! What great happiness! Our master will outlive all his relatives! " Then the sultan's face brightened and he said,

"Thank you, my friend. Go immediately with my treasurer to give you 50 gold coins. "

Along the way, the treasurer told the interpreter, "But you do not interpret the sultan's dream in a different way than the other interpreter!" With a sly smile, the clever man replied, "Remember that one can say many things: but it all depends on how he says them ..."

Elizabeth Lucas, Wisdom as Medicine

What is communication?

Effective communication is based on the ability to be able to express yourself appropriately both verbally and non-verbally. The pertinency is related to both the surrounding culture and the current situation. It covers the individual opportunity to express ourselves in relation to other people's opinions, desires, needs or even fears or, if necessary, to ask for advice or help.

Communication, therefore, means conveying messages. The sender sends a message and the recipient must decrypt that message. With good communication, the sent and received message match. In order to avoid misunderstandings in this transfer, it is important for the recipient to give feedback, ie. to explain how he deciphered the message, how it reached to him, and how it affected him.

In this way, the sender sees whether the result of the receipt coincides with the intention of the sender.

Each message has four levels: **Factual level**, **Relationship level**, **Self-disclosure level**, and **Appeal level**. Disruptions and misunderstandings occur primarily when the recipient and sender find different points and elements of the message for important.

1. **Factual level:** refers to the essential content of a message that the sender transmits to the recipient.

2. **Self-disclosure level:** shows what the sender reveals about himself. He inserts his identity and personality into the message sent.

3. **Relationship level:** expresses how the sender and recipient relate to

each other, what they think of each other. Non-verbal accompanying signals are often used here.

4. **Appeal level:** expresses the intention of the sender. Provides information about the purpose of the statement and what the sender wants to achieve.

Which aspect of the message will be perceived as the main one depends on the previous experience and expectations of the recipient and on the non-verbal signals of the sender or, respectively, on how the recipient interprets them. The level of relationship, the level of self-disclosure and the level of appeal are conveyed through facial expressions and gestures and voice expression, ie. nonverbal. Social competence, which begins at the factual level (content - dialogic conversation) expands to the level of the relationship with an interpersonal dimension. A basic prerequisite for effective communication is therefore the ability to accept and correctly interpret the behaviour of others - both nonverbally and verbally.

Violation of the relationship on a factual level means that a person is stuck there and neither factually nor humanly can move forward. Different cultures and levels of development have different rules about which emotional expression is appropriate for a particular social context. Knowing this is just as important for communicative competence as the ability to cognitively accept a point of view.

As each conversation consists of verbal and non-verbal elements, one coordination is needed to avoid misunderstandings. Congruence is therefore a prerequisite for successful communication.

In a person who is congruent, the content of the message coincides with body language and the auditory sub-qualities of the message. All communicative aspects, such as words, intonation or body language, match. They convey the same message. And incongruence means a contradiction, for example, between what is said and the behaviour.

Communication and perception form unity. Three processes should be distinguished in one communication process:

1. The process of **Perception**: for example, the perception of a look or a word or a gesture.
2. The process of **Interpretation**: what is perceived is filled with meaning. I can interpret a look as contemptuous, admiring, shameless, arrogant, greedy ... In these interpretations, we

are guided by our previous experience.

3. The process of **Feeling something**: According to how I will interpret the look, it will cause some corresponding feeling: irritation, joy, disappointment, shame, discomfort, anger etc.

The skill of leading a conversation

A good atmosphere between the partners in the conversation is also needed for factual, meaningful messages, successful in content. The task of a good conversation is, above all, to create a trusting relationship. Only on this basis can addressing substantive issues and resolving problems and conflicts be achieved.

When conducting a conversation, three criteria should be agreed upon whenever possible:

1. **Authenticity**: This represents harmony with oneself. Not to pretend, nor to suppress our feelings, nor to replay them, but to verbalize them.

2. **Acceptance**: This is the positive attitude towards the person opposite, "Yes" to his "I am". This does not exclude the possibility of constructive criticism concerning his behaviour.

3. **Empathy or compassion**: This is the ability to perceive others, empathize and give feedback.

Elements of positive conversation are diverse. We can start by physically, bodily facing our interlocutor. To have a calm but at the same time mobile body position. To maintain eye contact. To use an intonation that suggests yes to a friendly acceptance. In our arsenal, we need to have and use various gestures of approval, such as a smile, a nod of the head and others. Our whole personality can emit peace. Not to rush into the conversation, not hasten things, tolerating the pauses. To be able to ask constructive questions and show a lively interest. Our questions need to be understandable, as well as our answers. We need to express recognition and show respect all the time. When it is necessary to express sympathy and understanding.

Elements of negative conversation are also quite diverse. Quite often we can observe how the whole body of one of the interlocutors is turned to the other side. Eye contact is often interrupted and motor restlessness is observed, ie. a person moves a lot, he is impatient to finish the conversation, hasty, irritated. There may be a lack of interest and even boredom. Often part of a negative conversation is silence and reticence, lack of feedback, frequent interruptions, abrupt change of topic and aggressive, offensive criticism. It is not uncommon to see opposition and contradiction, reproaches, doubts, and objections, attempts to emphasise the other's mistakes. Very often the positive is not acknowledged and the position of arrogance is observed.

Techniques for leading a conversation

Active listening:

"Problems are generally as complex and multi-layered as the person who deals with them." (Leupold). Active listening has a number of positive effects on the conversation partner and makes it possible for the "recipient" to understand on a deeper level what the "sender" wants to tell him:

When this technique is used correctly, the interlocutor feels understood and accepted, does not have to defend himself, feels his right to express his feelings and feels that he is encouraged by the attentive listener to stand up and deal with his problems. Trust relationships are also built on the basis of which the interlocutors become more accessible to each other. There is also a higher willingness to compromise.

The basis for a constructive conversation is the approving attitude, which makes active listening possible. Only when the level of the relationship is clarified can messages on a factual level become effective. An important function of active listening is to reduce the pace of the conversation in order to allow the speaker to describe or, accordingly, to state his problem calmly and in detail. For the one who does not have to defend himself, because his point of view is not questioned, but is accepted, there is less danger of getting more and more entangled in his arguments. Active listening does not mean monotonous repetition of what the partner is saying in the conversation, but rather a complete concentration on the other person and stoppage of our own need to speak. In this way, we manage to be attentive to the essential, ie. the feelings, thoughts, experiences, fears, needs of the other. And so active listening is a starting point for communicating with people.

Paraphrasing:

This means the brief transmission of what is said in one's own words. By repeating, the other person is signalled that we are listening intensively and the partner in the conversation has the opportunity to perceive and express his thoughts and feelings even more clearly. It is important to emphasize either the feelings or the thoughts and the differentiated exposure of the external contents. With this technique, misunderstandings can be avoided from the very beginning. Paraphrasing does not mean that one agrees with the opinion heard. This is only about the correct understanding of what is said and the correct understanding of the other person.

Interpretation:

With this technique, what is available remains as it is, but it is given a different, often new meaning. For example, behaviours that are often perceived as an expression of "weakness" are defined as a sign of "strength." Unseen and unappreciated competencies can be derived from deficits.

Looping:

This technique is an approximation to the problem by using a summary of the information obtained so far and asking constructive questions in order to immerse yourself in the underlying levels of the problem.

Techniques for asking questions

"Only when we ask the right questions will
we find the right answers."
LF Wittgenstein

Questions have a very special function, place and significance in the process of communication. Through them, we can get information. They allow the correction of certain ideas and expectations. Very often a well-asked question reduces resistance and gives impetus to new perspectives. Through the right question, one discovers or rediscovers values and realities. The elegantly asked question shows that a person has an interest in something or someone and even feels respect. Having the right to ask questions is the basis of freedom. The question asked speaks of a person's personal responsibility and his self-determination as a subject of communication and life in general. Through questions, we explore the world and can encourage others to do the same. We are opening new fields of action and taking the initiative to change. One question can provoke the interlocutor in a positive direction.

In the process of mediation, there are many opportunities to ask questions. There are so-called introductory questions, which are asked at the beginning of the process. They are related to various topics that accompany mediation. There are also questions about information, such as: who, how, where and when. These questions have a high value for clarifying the specifics of the process and the underlying meanings. Clarifying questions are often used, which require specificity, such as

"What do you mean by all this?". Another type of question is checking-up questions, such as "Why do you think so? How will this ... work? " Of particular importance to the mediation process are hypothetical questions such as "If you had a choice, what would you do?". With their help, new thoughts arise, old beliefs are rethought and new horizons are opened.

Circular questioning:

The circular question is used to obtain information by looking for differences and conclusions. The questions asked to a person, what the other person might think and believe, serve to reveal thoughts and feelings. This way of asking questions can have a variety of purposes:

- To clarify the signs of differentiation and identification: (How do you know you are not depressed? What will you do differently then?)

- For merging qualities: (What behaviour should Dad show in order for Mom to think that he is depressed?)
- To introduce an external perspective through the triad questions: (What would Dad's mother say about their marriage?)
- To rank hierarchically: (Who cares most about Dad?)
- For coincidence and discrepancy: (What led to this joint decision?)
- To clarify the interactive impact of important life events and major changes: (How did your wife's decision come about?)
- To change the point of view: (What do you think was the reason for your wife's complaint, what does she want to achieve with this?)

- For explanations and hypotheses: (What would happen if ... Imagine that the children have already grown up, what would living together look like?)
- To clarify individual and family values: (What do you think about your wife's mental breakdown after the change of job?)
- To discover alternative realities: (How will you know that you feel accepted by your family?)

Closed questions:

This type of question requires a clear and precise answer, most often "Yes" or "No". Examples of such questions are:

- Can you confirm this?
- Do you want to agree with this proposal?

- Is this the only aspect you need to consider?

Open questions:

These should be questions that contain a question word, but this is not mandatory. This type of question can arise after asking a closed question, followed by the question "Why?". Open-ended questions open up different answers, suggest nothing, and do not aim for a specific answer. Examples of such questions are:

- What do you want to decide today and here?
- What do you think about this?
- How can this solve the problem?

For optimal communication, it is useful to give the other person as much freedom of action and free space in his response as possible. That is why it is important in mediation to work with open questions, but not in such a way that they are only questions with a question word, but to be such questions in which the mediator has an open attitude towards the participants in the mediation. We understand whether some questions are correct only when their answers are available.

The body language:

The body responds to thoughts, emotions and situations. Therefore, in any kind of interaction, the partner in the conversation must "keep an eye" so that a mutual reaction of body language is possible. To observe means that someone is perceived, even when he is a passive listener. Eye contact allows for the reception of signals. In this way, one can react to them verbally. In the form of a "hypothesis", it is asked whether body language has been understood. For example: "I could imagine that you feel like this at the moment ... I think you are a little ... at the moment ..." and so on.

"Reflecting team"

Reflecting team is a method which roots can be found in the systematic form of therapy. Tom Andersen, a Norwegian social psychiatrist, developed this form of intervention. He examined the usual ways of communicating and intervening and suggested, as an alternative, an "observation system" whose focus in terms of therapy should be on the Here and Now. The type of communication is reflective and pursues the goal of creating free space to learn new perspectives, content and opportunities for a solution. In the reflecting team method, people tell their stories in a therapeutic situation in the presence of real other people. Participating systems go through a common process alternating directed and undirected communication. For example, the participants in the therapeutic team take a reflective position and follow the conversation in the consultation (directed communication). They do not participate in the conversation, but only listen carefully. In a certain way, the positions change. The participants from the reflecting team talk about the heard and observed from the process of conversation (undirected communication). The previous system listens to the conversation about the conversation. Mediators in the mediation process take a reflective position.

Historical course:

- The advice-seekers are interviewed by a consultant. The reflecting team usually also sits in the same room and does not interfere in the interview but listens in silence. The interviewing team asks the reflecting team for their ideas after a while.

- Then the participants in the team share their perceptions, observations, questions. During this time, they do not make contact (not even eye contact) with the interviewing team in any way. This approach allows the participants in the interview system (client plus consultant) during the hearing to let the views of the team members influence them and then to be able to process them for themselves.

- After the reflecting team is over, the participants in the interview system talk about their ideas about the reflections. Therefore, they have "a conversation about the reflecting team's conversation of the interview system's conversation."

Changing positions:

The reflecting team is a special kind of conversation in which Andersen distinguishes two dialogues. He calls the exchange of mutual observations, ideas, thoughts of communicating people an external dialogue. The internal dialogue takes place at the same time. During the conversation, everyone decides for themselves which content is important and which should be recorded. The division of verbal, experiential and listening, reflective position is the main idea of the reflecting team. The listener participates only in the internal dialogue and thus experiences the reflection of others from a distance and can from this position consider new aspects and rethink without having to justify himself. "Conversations need pauses that are enough for a person to think about the process of the conversation. And they have to go slow enough so that the mind has enough time to choose the ideas it wants to join and find the words that can express that connection. ”(Andersen). The interviewer can ask for the ideas of the reflecting team - but the reflecting team can also say by itself that they have valuable ideas to say. In this case, the interviewer and his conversation partners decide if they want to hear something and when. The reflecting team usually speaks for five to ten minutes, sometimes longer. Usually, it is not interrupted by the interviewing system. Then the interviewing system speaks again and the reflecting team listens.

Finally, the interviewer asks the following questions:
- Which was important?
- Which was good not to tell?
- What was missing?

The interview system can be, for example, a family plus a counsellor. This system talks or is interviewed by the consultant. This is called directed communication. The therapist or counsellor often asks unusual but very accurate and appropriate questions and thus gathers information, allowing each family member to describe his or her own view of things. The advice-seeking system has the freedom to accept the ideas of the reflecting team or to reject them, as well as not listening to them at all if desired. The therapist or counsellor makes sure that each person of the advice-seeking system can express their own opinion and discuss the information provided. He often uses questions such as, "Is there anything you want to say in what you heard?", "Was there something you didn't agree with or something that we shouldn't have talked about?", "Is there something missing according to you? " The conversation or interview ends with a discussion of the clients' wishes for the future.

An observation system or so-called reflecting team monitors and keeps notes, listens carefully to the thoughts, plans and interpretations of the family (which is the advice-seeking system), without having to immediately take a certain position. This system tries to reflect what the advice-seeking system says. The monitoring system listens carefully and does not speak directly to the advice-seeking system, look carefully for different opinions for the purpose of enrichment, not for the purpose of questioning. It aims to observe and perceive both the approving context and the confrontational harsh statements.

The rules in the reflecting team:

- While the reflecting team is listening, it does not interrupt the interviewer.
- During the listening, each member of the team keeps his thoughts and ideas to himself.
- During the reflection, the reflecting team exchanges their thoughts only with each other and in no way makes contact with the interviewing system, not even eye contact.
- Reflecting on thoughts is about the variety of possible points of view, not the best idea.
- Respect for those seeking advice is at the forefront.
- The questions should be formulated carefully, for example, "Is it possible to ...?"
- Non-verbal models should also be used.

- The expressed ideas should encourage the process of reflection, but should still be understandable and applicable to the client, ie. "Appropriately unusual."
- Topics that one of the advice-seekers does not want to be discussed are not covered.
- It is talked about only what is directly related to the interview.
- No edifying advice is given.

Methodological competence:

The feedback from the reflecting team must be in the form of a dialogue and does not represent an exposure of positions. Only in this way can a variety of perspectives arise. Different members of the reflecting team have different points of view and help to broaden the horizons. They give a new perspective on the problem. Therefore, the task of the reflecting team is not to seek solutions but to present opportunities. Smart advices, monologues and "muttering" are prevented by respecting the person and what is heard. Here we must remember that everything perceived is subjective, that an individual is able to use his personal resources to deal with the problems, that the one affected is, in fact, the expert of his own decision. Personal ideas are not always applicable and universal in every case. People are prone to change when they feel valued.

The reflecting team can perform various activities and have various functions, such as supervision, the pedagogical process of training and learning, to perform systematic therapies, colleague consultation or mediation. **In supervision**, the problem is precisely defined and conveyed in words. The reflecting team is activated more often and at shorter intervals and is led by the advice-seekers themselves. **The pedagogical process of learning** helps with communication problems and other difficulties in group processes. This is a feedback method. **In systematic therapies**, the reflecting team remains invisible to others but can be heard. **In the collegial consultation**, the reflecting team is involved in an effective, clearly structured interaction process of processing and solving problems in the field of professional activity.

Dr Ed. Watzke (Hans-Joachim Watzke) says: "Together with a colleague and through the reflecting team, I introduced a scene in which customers become an audience. The co-mediators sit on the stage, so to speak, and lead a discourse there. The discourse of the various possible realities! The reflecting team is presented as a kind of free-associating, fantasizing, uncensored vocal thinking, testing, feeling, etc. I share with the client, we allow ourselves to fantasize and think out loud about everything that passes through our heart and mind ... the clients listen, and the mediators help their unconscious to manifest. This method gives us the opportunity to find space, to open our thoughts, to discover opportunities, because now on the stage there is a dialogue or a discourse, which in the way of its presentation is not a reality and also does not want to be, but only to spread opportunities ... ".

Small group work
Practical exercise

Small group A

This small group (of three people) develops questions to be asked by one selected participant in the interview phase. The following catalogue of questions is useful for compiling such questions. It focuses on solution-oriented questions and circular questions that are used in systematic consultation situations.

Possible questions to start the process:

- What should we talk about in this conversation in any cases?
- If there are more desires/problems, which of them is most important to you?
- On a scale from 0 to 10, where 10 is the highest value, how big do you

estimate your workload with this problem?

- What would be the worst thing that could happen if nothing changed in the problem?
- What would person "X" say if I asked him about the problem?
- What would the person "X" for whom we are talking about now think if he were here listening to us?
- How do you explain that things are as they are?
- Who thinks the same way and who thinks differently?
- How could this be explained?
- Are there periods in which you can successfully deal with the problem?
- When does the problem occur less frequently or not at all?

- What needs to happen to increase your confidence in the possible solutions?
- How specifically will you notice that the problem has been solved?
- Imagine that nothing will change in the problem in the long run! What implications will this have for you?
- Assuming you decide on "A" (hypothetical decision), what will be the consequences?
- In our preliminary exercises, an absolutely crazy idea was born. Assuming you do "A" (which is something absolutely crazy), what would happen?
- Do you want to answer another question that I have not asked so far?
- Do you think what we have discussed so far has been helpful to you?

- Which questions do you think could be more useful than the ones asked so far?

Small group B

This group is actually the reflecting team. You need to distribute the responsibilities among the members of this group, ie. who pays attention to what and for what every person observes. The monitoring criteria can be the following:

- The non-verbal behaviour of the advice-seekers.

- Mental comparison with "similar" cases.

- The metaphorical statements of the advice-seekers.

- Development of models for an explanation.

- Considering exceptions and introducing new ideas and perspectives.

Three easy steps in the practical exercises:

1. **The phase of the interview** - One participant from group A interviews the advice-seekers, orienting himself by the questions that have been previously compiled in the group.
2. **The reflecting team** - After the interview phase, the reflecting team sits in a circle for short reflection phase in such a way that the gaze is not straight directed on the advice-seekers and so this process could be observed "from the outside". During the interview, the participants in the interview had been keeping notes that they can now use. The phase is

introduced if possible with a positive additional meaning of the process.

3. **Feedback from the advice-seekers** - They provide feedback about the course of supervision.

Final Words

Thanks to everyone who was interested in this book. I hope each of you has been able to bring out the needed knowledge so that you can help both yourself and the people you love.

9 798689 072715